How Coding Works

by Ben Hubbard

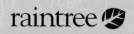

raintree

a Capstone company — publishers for children

Raintree is an imprint of Capstone Global Library Limited, a company incorporated in England and Wales having its registered office at 264 Banbury Road, Oxford, OX2 7DY – Registered company number: 6695582

www.raintree.co.uk
myorders@raintree.co.uk

Edited by Nikki Potts
Designed by Sarah Bennett
Picture research by Ruth Smith
Production by Laura Manthe
Originated by Capstone Global Library Limited
Printed and bound in China

ISBN 978 1 4747 3500 1
20 19 18 17 16
10 9 8 7 6 5 4 3 2 1

British Library Cataloguing in Publication Data
A full catalogue record for this book is available from the British Library.

Acknowledgements
We would like to thank the following for permission to reproduce photographs: Getty Images: Bloomberg, 12, 13; iStockphoto: DragonImages, 10, back cover left; Shutterstock: Angela Waye, 22 (surfing), Jason Winter, 9, Levent Konuk, 15, 22 (diagram), Monkey Business Images, 21, 22 (instruction), Nikolaeva, cover design element, interior design element, OlegDoroshin, 7, Ollyy, 8, photovibes, 5, ProStockStudio, cover, Rawpixel.com, 4, 6, 11, 18, 19, 22 (algorithm), (programmer), back cover right, studio0411, 14, Thongchai Kitiyanantawong, 17, wavebreakmedia, 20, 22 (task), welcomia, 16

We would like to thank Matt Anniss for his invaluable help in the preparation of this book.

Every effort has been made to contact copyright holders of material reproduced in this book. Any omissions will be rectified in subsequent printings if notice is given to the publisher.

All the internet addresses (URLs) given in this book were valid at the time of going to press. However, due to the dynamic nature of the internet, some addresses may have changed, or sites may have changed or ceased to exist since publication. While the author and publisher regret any inconvenience this may cause readers, no responsibility for any such changes can be accepted by either the author or the publisher.

Contents

Some words are shown in bold, **like this**.
You can find them in the glossary on page 22.

How do computers work?

Computers can do many complicated things. They follow **instructions** to complete **tasks**.

Computers only do what they are told. People provide the instructions.

What are programs?

A program is a set of **instructions** that a computer follows. Computers need programs for every **task** they do.

Programs allow us to **surf** the internet, learn new things or even play games. Computers could not do anything without programs.

What is code?

Computer programs are written in code.
A computer's basic language is called
"machine code".

Machine code is a series of the numbers "0" and "1". It is a language you can learn like any other.

What is coding?

Giving a computer a set of step-by-step **instructions** is called "coding".

Programmers write a set of instructions in code that humans can understand. The computer then turns these instructions into machine code.

What is coding like?

Coding tells a computer what to do.
These **instructions** can be as simple as
"wait 5 seconds" and "play sound".

Computers only do what they are told.
They cannot think for themselves.

What is an algorithm?

An **algorithm** is a list of coding steps for a computer program. Coding steps must be in the correct order for a program to work.

Programmers often draw a **diagram** of their algorithm. This helps them make sure the steps are in order.

What are some coding languages?

There are many coding languages. Each one is used to create different types of programs.

```
155
156
                    suffix:    '.min'
                }) : gutil.noop())
                .pipe( isProduction ? gulp.dest( pa
159                 .pipe( isProduction ? gutil.noop() : b
160
161        });
162
163        // JS
164    gulp.task('js', function() {
165        var scriptBase = gulp.src( basePaths.scr
166            .pipe($.plumber({
167                errorHandler: function (err) {
168                    new gutil.PluginError('JS B
169                    this.emit('end');
170
171                }
172            }))
173            .pipe($.concat('ui-base.js'))
174            .pipe(isProduction ? gulp.dest( p
175
176        var scriptVendorBase = gulp.src( ba
177            .pipe($.plumber({
178                errorHandler: function (err
179                    new gutil.PluginError('
                     this.emit('end');
```

Javascript

Games and websites are types of
programs. Some common coding
languages are Scratch, Python,
Java, C, PHP and Javascript.

How are coding languages different?

Each coding language has its own rules. The rules say which words and numbers should be used in a code language.

Programs will not work if the wrong words or numbers are used. Code can look strange at first. But many coding languages are easy to learn.

How do I become a programmer?

There are many ways to become a **programmer**. Your school or community centre may teach coding classes. You can also learn from books and the internet.

Ask an adult to help you try the coding websites at the end of this book.

Glossary

 **algorithm** a list of steps a programmer gives a computer to perform a task or solve a problem

 **diagram** simple drawing that shows how something works

 **instruction** command or order telling something or someone to do something

 **programmer** person who writes computer programs

 **surfing** moving from website to website on the internet to look for something

 **task** piece of work to be done

Find out more

Books

Computer Coding Made Easy, Carol Vordeman (DK, 2014)

Lift-the-Flap: Computers and Coding, Rosie Dickens (Usborne, 2015)

Understanding Programming and Logic (Understanding Computing), Matthew Anniss (Raintree, 2016)

Websites

moshi.kano.me/#
This Kano website lets kids code their own Pong game.

uk.code.org/learn
This Code UK website provides simple coding tutorials, including building a Star Wars galaxy.

www.bbc.co.uk/guides/zqnc4wx
This BBC website explains simple coding for young learners.

Index